CELL THEORY
FOR
SMARTYPANTS

Anushka Ravishankar

ILLUSTRATED BY

Pia Alizé Hazarika

duckbill

An imprint of Penguin Random House

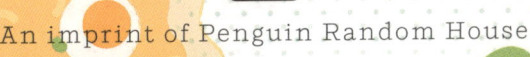

DUCKBILL BOOKS

USA | Canada | UK | Ireland | Australia
New Zealand | India | South Africa | China | Singapore

Duckbill Books is part of the Penguin Random House group of companies
whose addresses can be found at global.penguinrandomhouse.com

Published by Penguin Random House India Pvt. Ltd
4th Floor, Capital Tower 1, MG Road,
Gurugram 122 002, Haryana, India

Penguin
Random House
India

First published in Duckbill Books by
Penguin Random House India 2024

ISBN 9780143461050

Typeset in Weiss by Digiultrabooks Pvt. Ltd
Printed at Thomson Press India Ltd, New Delhi

www.penguin.co.in

CELL THEORY states that:

All organisms are composed of one or more cells. The cell is the basic unit of structure and organization in an organism. All cells come from pre-existing cells.

Every plant and every animal is made up of tiny little **cells**.

Plant and animal cells are so small that they cannot be seen by the human eye. You need a **microscope** to see them.

I KNOW YOU HAVE SHARP EYES, BUT EVEN YOU CAN'T SEE CELLS.

YES, THEY EXIST.

YES, I'M SURE. PEOPLE HAVE SEEN THEM THROUGH A MICROSCOPE.

When you look at any part of a plant or animal through a microscope, you can see they are made up of cells.

ANIMAL CELL

PLANT CELL

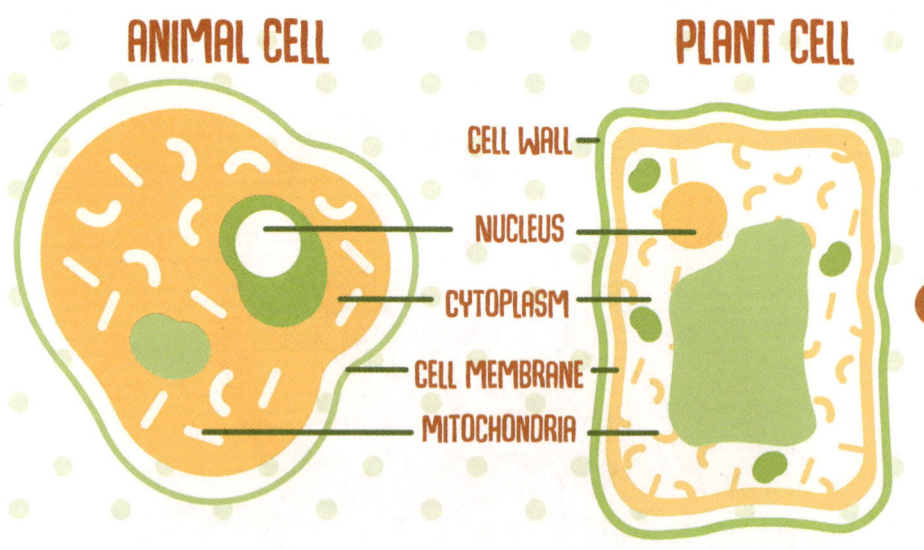

CELL WALL

NUCLEUS

CYTOPLASM

CELL MEMBRANE

MITOCHONDRIA

Cells are made up of different parts.
Every part of the cell has a job to do.

The **cell membrane** is like a fence, but also like a gate. As a fence, it keeps things inside the cell. As a gate, it lets things in and out of the cell.

Plant cells have a **cell wall** outside the cell membrane.

INSIDE

OUTSIDE

PLANT CELL

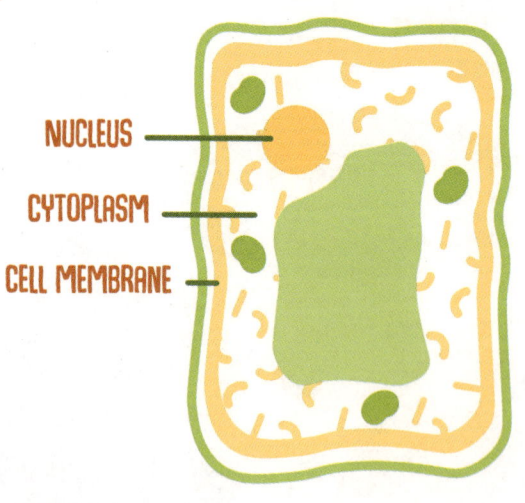

NUCLEUS

CYTOPLASM

CELL MEMBRANE

Inside the cell membrane is a liquid called **cytoplasm**. There are many floating bodies in the cytoplasm. These are called **organelles**.

There are many different organelles in the cytoplasm, and each of them has a separate job. Some of the organelles are **mitochondria**, **Golgi bodies** and **chloroplasts**.

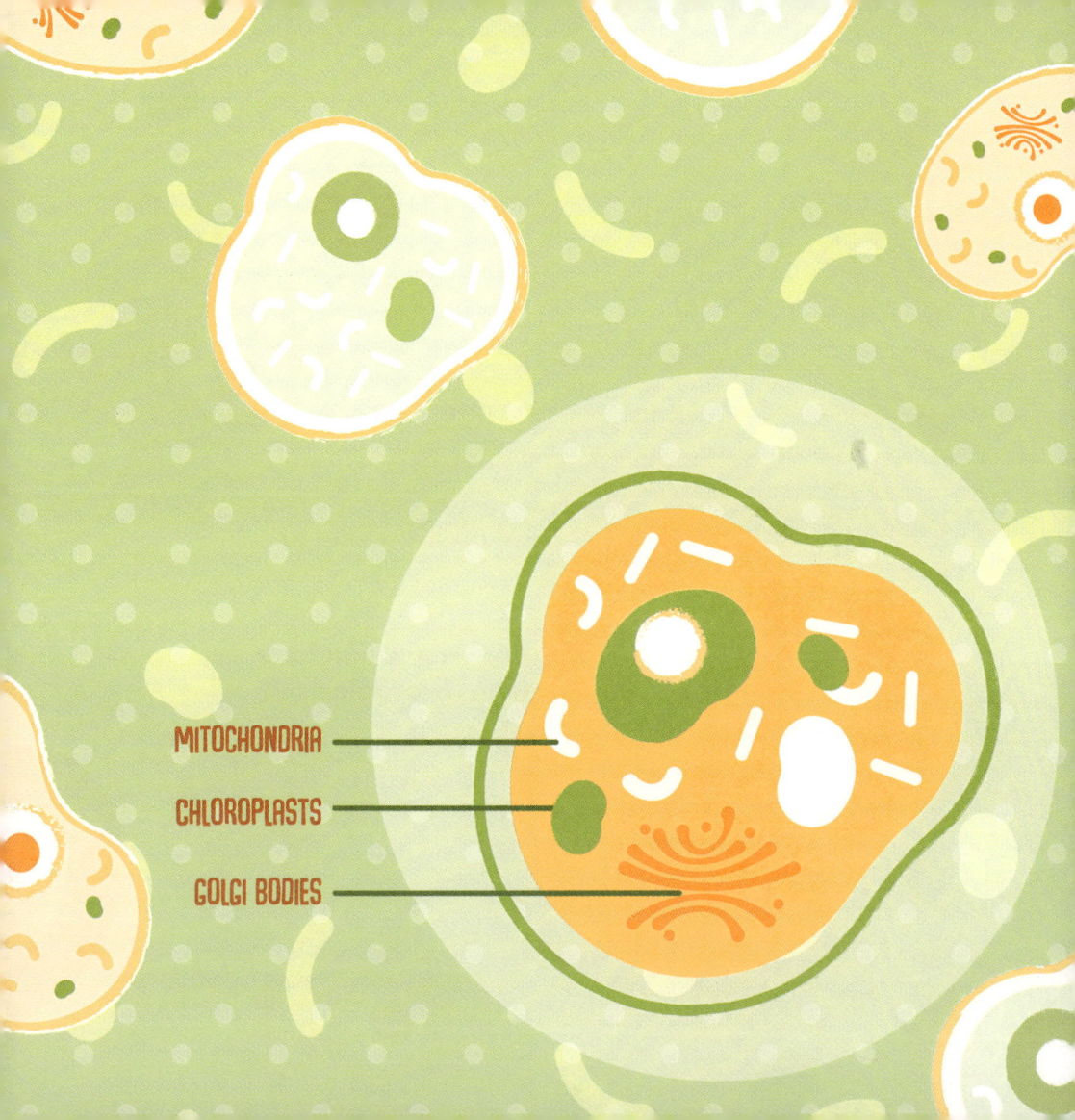

MITOCHONDRIA

CHLOROPLASTS

GOLGI BODIES

Mitochondria makes energy.

Golgi bodies package up the waste to send out of the cell.

Plant cells have chloroplasts which help make food. There are no chloroplasts in animal cells.

The **nucleus** is a ball-like thing in the cell.

It is also an organelle. Inside the nucleus are **chromosomes** and the **nucleolus**.

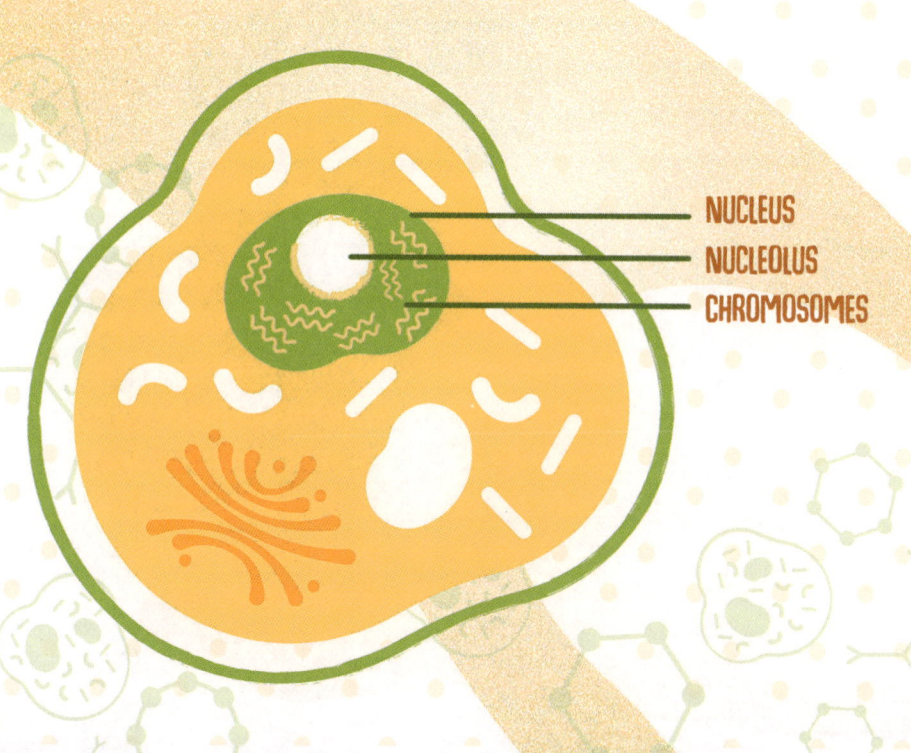

NUCLEUS

NUCLEOLUS

CHROMOSOMES

The nucleus is like the main office of the cell. And the nucleolus is the boss, which decides what the cell should do.

For example, it decides what the cell membrane should allow in and what it should throw out.

NUCLEUS

CYTOPLASM

MITOCHONDRIA

CHLOROPLAST

NUCLEUS

CYTOPLASM

MITOCHONDRIA

Different cells of the plant or animal do different jobs.

What the job is depends on where the cell is.

Cells in the roots of plants absorb water and minerals. Cells in the leaves make food through photosynthesis.*

YES, LIKE IN A HOME.

THE WATCHMAN AT THE GATE CHECKS WHO COMES AND GOES.

OHO! IT'S YOUR JOB TO EAT?

THE COOK IN THE KITCHEN MAKES FOOD.

NICE TRY. IT'S NOT TIME FOR TREATS.

* *Photosynthesis for Smartypants*

One of the jobs of cells is to give shape and support to the animal or plant.

Cells are like bricks that give shape to a house.

The things that the plant or animal needs are brought in through the cells.

In plants, the cells help with photosynthesis.

In animals, the cells help absorb food that the animal eats.

The cells also do the job of getting rid
of waste inside the plant or animal.

One cell can break up or become many cells in different ways. For example, they might break up so that one cell becomes two, two become four and so on.

When the number of cells increases, it helps the plant or animal grow.

Plant cells have a firm structure because of the cell wall.

Animal cells are blobby and shapeless.

Some creatures, like the amoeba, have only one cell.

Cats have sixty to eighty million cells!

Anushka Ravishankar likes
science, cats and books, not
necessarily in that order. So
she decided to write a book to
explain science to a cat. The cat
doesn't always get the point,
but she hopes her readers will.

Pia Alizé Hazarika is an illustrator primarily interested in comics and visual narratives.

Her independent and collaborative work has been published by Penguin Random House India (The PAO Anthology), Comix India, Manta Ray Comics, The Pulpocracy, Captain Bijli Comics, Yoda Press, Zubaan Books and the Khoj Artists Collective. She runs PIG Studio, an illustration-driven space, based out of New Delhi.

Her handle on Instagram is @_PigStudio_.

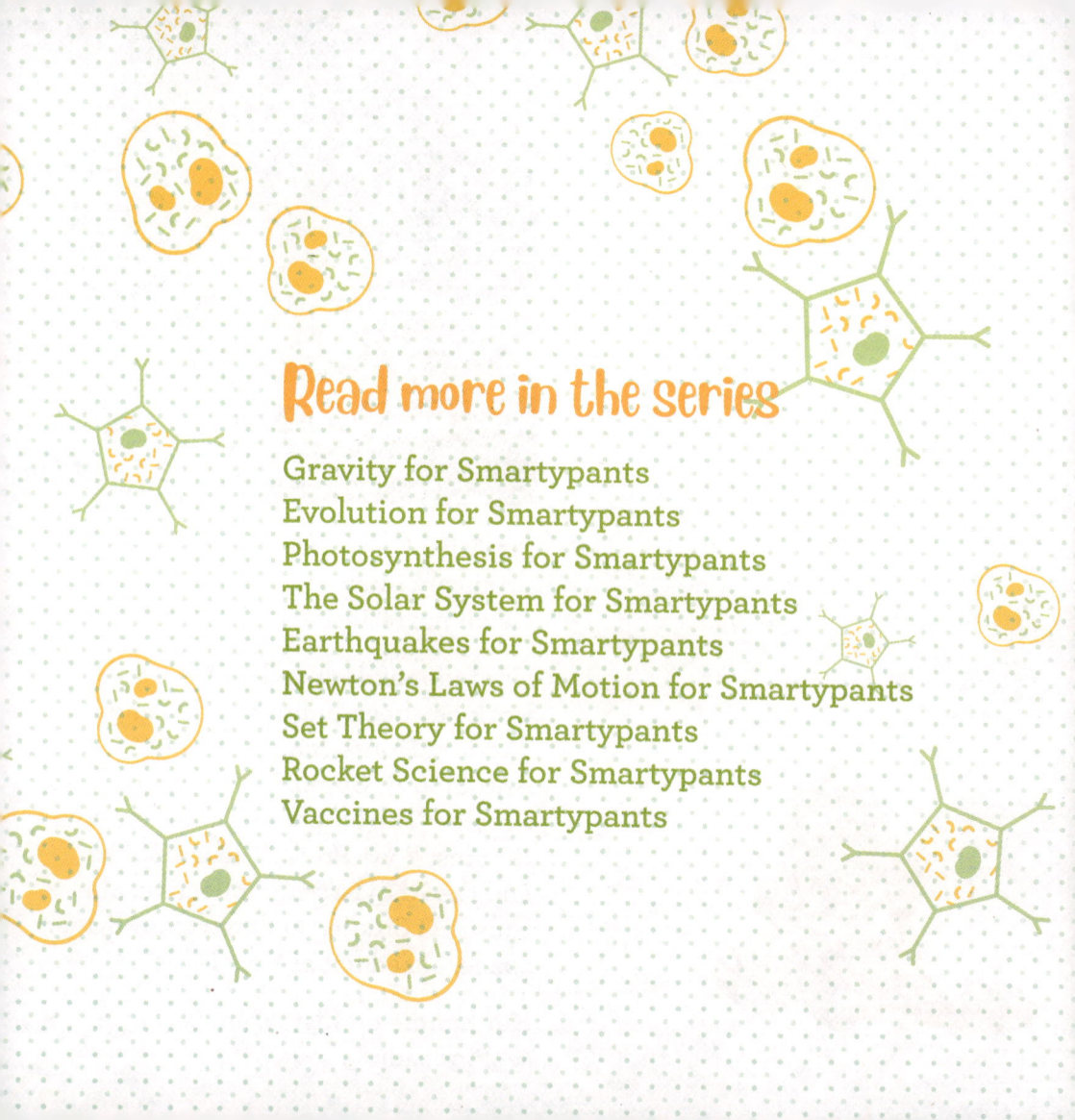

Read more in the series